From a Brother to Another

My Path to Christ in Prose and Verse

Glenn Schuler

Copyright © 2022 by Glenn Schuler

All rights reserved.

No portion of this book may be reproduced in any form without written permission from the publisher or author, except as permitted by U.S. copyright law.

DEDICATION

To my earthly father, George Schuler, who passed away in 2021.
My father was a humble man with not a lot to say.
An enlarged heart, a life of struggles,
Yet content with all his days.
A larger heart was needed to contain all of his love.
Sent from his Heavenly Father from heaven up above.
Recalling my days with him moving to manhood.
He never shirked from any task.
He did everything he could to teach us about duty
And what is most important.
Walking down upon this earth
We have always felt supported.
Our God above gave him his strength.
We need to learn this too.
Thank you, dear Lord, for this great man.
We send him back to you.

ACKNOWLEDGMENTS

Special thanks to Marilyn Buttjer, who helped me learn to appreciate the value of an English teacher and of punctuation.

Alpha Writers, a local group that helped me keep the creative fires burning.

Pastor Michael Downey and my home church family he leads.

Bev, who has offered her support and love through all my various endeavors.

Hidden Acres Christian Retreat, for providing a wonderful place to receive inspiration.

Mostly, Lord Jesus, who makes all things possible.

contents

Tapestry	1
Introduction	2
Gifts	4
Alphabet	5
Chapter 1 Youth	6
Pearl	8
Give	9
Romantics	10
Free	11
Canned Courage	12
Happiness	13

Sunset	14
Chapter 2 Finding Love	15
Worth	17
Mystery	18
Off-Colored Shade	19
Treasure	20
Steps	21
Forgive	22
No Thanks	23
Summit	24
Chapter 3 Dark Days	25
Blame	27
Garden	28
Cold Heart	29
Ghosts	30
Freedom	31
Guilty Heart	32
Trojan Horse	33
Converse	34

Lone Wolf	35
DC and ME	36
Pity Me	37
My Day	38
Lust	39
Junk	40
Hidden	41
Chapter 4 Rebound	42
Sunshine and Rain	44
Burning Bridges	45
Mighty Oak	46
Maker	47
One-Man Cart	48
Child's Toy	49
Get Your Way	50
Friends	51
Strayed	52
Blind	53
What's Left	54
One Up, One Down	55

Sharing	56
Behind A Cloud	57
Pet Sin	59
Chapter 5 Loving Again	60
First Glimpse	62
Late Love	63
View	64
Discovered	65
Comfortable	66
True	67
Changed Plans	68
Fly	69
Well	70
Gift Package	71
Total	72
Reading Minds	73
New Start	74
My Eyes	75
Sleepless	76
Gold	77

Fear	78
Butterfly	79
Giver	80
Wood	81
Drama	82
My Wife, The Giver	83
Fixer	84
Paths Crossed	85
Vision	86
Trust	87
Old Story	88
Scared	89
Your Flowers	90
My Name	91
Wedding Ring	92
Lovely Woman	93
Chapter 6 God's True Nature	94
Train To Salvation	96
God's Clock	97
Traveler	98

Grandpa	99
Wedding Feast	100
Never Alone	101
God's New Vessel	102
God Loved Us First	103
Little Fruit	104
The Lord's Arms	105
Creator	106
Teeter Totter	107
God's Johnny Appleseed	108
Vengeance	109
Path	110
Heaven's Hound	111
The End	112
Distance	113
Break The Chains	114
Doctor	115
Teacher	116
Chapter 7 The New Walk	117
About the author	119

Tapestry

Our life is the back of a tapestry God weaves now.
Masses of colored strings make a picture. How?
The beauty is concealed while we are living here.
We are tiny points of color on this side yet unclear.
One day we will pass over to the other side,
To see the artwork clearly when He provides a view.
Marveling with great wonder at how He stitched it all together.
Enjoying the beauty of His work in Heaven,
Now forever.

INTRODUCTION

I am nobody special. My life has been as ordinary as ordinary can be. There have been difficult times and times of plenty. We all discover things about ourselves as our story comes together.

Welcome to my story, which contains entertaining details—though some of them are not necessary for the purpose of this book. My desire is to share my great discovery, which was revealed to me as my life unfolded. It is a discovery you will make as well. My goal is to help you solve this mystery—not with a giant novel like *War and Peace*—but with poems inspired to show the feelings different episodes of life invoke.

We all come into this world naked, needy, and with no idea what is happening. God's purpose in creating us is to set us in motion on a path to find him. He is not hiding, though we may not see him right away. He is not powerless, yet we may not feel His hands upon us. He is not loveless; however, at times, we feel alone.

Let me take you with me in a different way—through my life and story. My plan is to give you enough context that you can relate to my feelings. These verses have come from loneliness, pain, joy,

2

revelation, misery, and even jail. They have come from living. Your story is more important to me than mine is. Please think of your life as you travel with me. I found God, not the God I would have made for myself, but the true God. He wants you to find Him too—not by force but by choice.

I could do nothing else once my heart was open to His love. This came by living a life as normal as any other, probably like yours. Thank you for letting me share mine. See how it matches yours, and then open your heart. God can be a part of your life. Actually, He is, whether you believe it or not. My prayer and purpose of this work is that you will believe. Enjoy.

GIFTS

God, as you choose to let me breathe,
Thank you for the gifts I received.
For your desire that I use them
To bring your kingdom glory.
That my flesh would choose to waste them
Would be a dismal story.
With joy, we watch You set the rules.
Providing all your glorious tools,
Hand in hand, we join the race.
Your divine knowledge sets the pace.
The Spirit powers up our souls.
Your Holy purpose as our goal.
1 Corinthians 7:7

ALPHABET

Twenty-six letters in the alphabet.
Since our youth, we know them well.
Mix them up with life and love, and our stories start to gel.
God only knows the number these little letters have to say.
Columns, novels, "posty" notes— each of us has his way.
For me, a rhyming poem is the way to get it out.
These little letters used just right. My verse may all but shout!
Proverbs 25:11

CHAPTER 1

Youth

I was lonely. As a boy without any knowledge or training in athletics, sports did not appeal to me. My dad and I did not throw balls of any type back and forth. My fondest memories were out in the woods with the .22 rifle, looking for careless squirrels to bring home to turn into the most delicious squirrel potpie.

Then we moved into a new area where baseball was everything and I knew nothing. To help me out, my new friends made special rules for me. Whatever side chose me last allowed me a position out by the monkey bars, far enough away that no second grader—unless they were on steroids—would ever hit a ball to me. This also gave me the privilege to come in or not when innings changed—whatever caused that to happen.

Instead of feeling hurt or sad or allowing the bullying to beat me, I chose to beat them to the punch. I chose to become the "comedian." This would give me the jump on them. If I made fun of myself first by my choice, how could their barbs hurt me?

My happiest moments were lying in the summer grass with my cousins, looking up at the stars in wonder, hoping a UFO or other marvel would appear to give us answers to what life was all about. Do you wonder at times why you exist or what purpose your life will serve? Walk with me through mine. There, perhaps, an answer lies.

I do know one person who seemed to have the answers—my paternal grandmother. She was an amazing woman. She lost her husband, my grandfather, when he was thirty-nine. She went on to raise four children on fifty dollars a month social security, plus what she earned as a housekeeper for some local people.

I was "appointed" to spend a week with Grandma each summer, after growing to the point my labors would be a benefit to her. She was all in for Jesus, never pushing it on me but always eager to answer any questions I would have.

I have no doubt that she awaits my arrival in heaven, because, in her private moments, she prayed with all her might for those she loved.

God, I think, has a sense of humor. He will probably send Grandma to greet me with her on-the-lips juicy kiss, still wearing her "lady mustache." I no doubt would not be there but for her ministry to me. Her most common statement, when hearing any complaints or doubts from anyone, was: "Take it to the Lord in prayer." She did.

pearl

Feeling like a pearl, lovely to see, only from sand I came to be.
Learning early to make chums laugh aloud,
Clearing the air of that lonely cloud.
Learning to listen to others share dreams
Made me feel important; for a moment, I gleam.
Doing what I could to fix what was broken
Meant volumes to me, was often a token.
To those on the outside, I may look quite grand,
Yet on the inside, I still feel the sand.
Still needing layers to soothe old feelings
That may never mend, may always be healing.
Proverbs 14:1

GIVE

He wandered the playground alone and afraid.
His young heart quite troubled, his self-worth not made.
He longed to be loved, not knowing yet how.
Needing it always, wanting it now.
The years drifted by, and lonely did pass.
When out of the stars there came such a lass.
With love to provide his hungry, low soul.
Never it seemed was there ever a toll.
The love was provided but with time seemed to wane.
When at last there was none to remain.
A lesson was learned by our poor lonely boy.
When at last he had found the source of his joy.
It is not love received when we're here to live.
It's how much we love when we set out to give.

John 13: 34-35
Proverbs 18:1

ROMANTICS

There is a name for types like mine
Who lay their hearts out on the line.
Hopeless romantics we would be.
It's through our hearts we seem to see.
We speak the language of the heart
And cannot stop once we start.
Matthew 12:34
Proverbs 27:19

Free

Love is free, made without price.
To gather it in would indeed be quite nice.
However, it must have some place to start
From deep within a caring heart.
Don't let fear or pride hold you down.
Reach inside—pass some around.
John 3:16+15:12

canned courage

To drown the teenage doubt and fear
Took only six cheap beers.
Pouring quenching fluid on a young soul's needs and fears.
Calming fog concealed the doubts, granting instant courage.
Gaining power from a can at a much too-early age.
Years march by, the truth comes out
That not a thing is solved.
Crawling down into the can, issues unresolved.
More times than not, with poor control,
The list of woes will grow.
Our Savior's blood and living water
Is the only way to go.
Proverbs 23:21

Happiness

There is a place called happiness,
No map to lead you there.
No travel guide, no rail to ride, no place to buy a fare.
The only mode of transport is somewhere in your mind.
But even then, it can be hard to find.
Begging, wanting, pushing hides it more.
Just go about your living;
It's behind the next door.
Psalms 68:3

sunset

A beautiful sunset. Oh, what a sight.
Most of us miss them, our timing not right.
If you happen to be at the right time to view,
You know what happens. You stop what you do.
Everything's forgotten for a moment of time.
Savor that moment. Enjoy the sublime.
Nothing else matters at that moment. It can't.
Sunsets are fleeting; time may be scant.
Romans 1:20

You made it through childhood, yet you may still have a hole in your heart. What do we need to fill this hole? Perhaps someone next to us will give us the love we crave. Let's go now and find someone.

CHAPTER 2

Finding Love

We have a human desire to seek love. No man is an island. Almost everyone has heard that. As you know, my heart was lonely. Most of the time I worked alone. A task was given, and off I would go to accomplish this task. I was reliable. Dad taught me to do the job required, then do a little more that was not expected. For example, I hired out to do some cultivating. After completing the task, I returned to the machine shed to park the tractor inside. At that point, I could have simply left and gone home, as I had done the job.

Instead, I swept out the cab and found some rags and water to clean the windows. Oh, and by the way, I fueled it up for the next day. See my point? Never was I without work to do for others.

For some reason, the praise I received for my efforts fell short. Why did I feel guilty? I knew who I was: a greedy manipulative youngster who would cash my check, buy some beer, party, and seek out someone to love me. It was hopeless to continue on my usual course. But what must I do?

I prayed. To this God my grandmother seemed to know so well. Dad took me to church almost every Sunday. I had my confirmation Bible I tried so hard to read. My prayer was, "If You do indeed exist, would You help me change? My life does not seem to be pointing in a good direction."

He did answer. Shortly after my efforts to change were in danger, a girl entered the picture. She also wanted change in her life, and we seemed to be good for each other. This distraction changed my life, pointing it in a better direction. Feeling that this was not just a coincidence, we decided to marry. Looking back, one could plead the case that this may have been a mistake, as we were still quite young.

In God's eyes, this was a path that would teach me many lessons of great value later.

As you heard, my father taught me early how to work hard. He showed me by his example. Among the men he worked with, he was the go-to guy—the first to climb the silo to attach the filling tube, sixty feet up with no safety harness. He was "superman" to me, yet I never knew his thoughts of me. He was a man of few words but what he did say was true. To this day—he is eighty-seven, and I am sixty-four—I have never caught him lying.

Remember how I talked about my grandmother's nature before? This was his mother. I must assume he suffers from the same thing you and I do. Approval from man falls short. We will never get enough praise from other men to overcome our knowledge of ourselves. Guilt is a blessing if you have the courage to face it.

My father also told me: "I cannot be with you to change what you may do. If you find yourself in trouble, you can get yourself out." Trouble did follow as the song lyrics go: "Looking for love in all the wrong places." We seek approval from everyone, yet only our Creator's approval counts. Where are you in your quest for love?

WOrTH

"What are you worth?" the world did say.
I do not know; I've not had my way.
He then set out to prove his "worth" to all the people
Of the earth, pleasing people of all classes.
Strangers, leaders, all the masses.
Losing sight of what's been given
To make this life worth living.
Those most important in his life—
His children and a loving wife.
Matthew 16:26
John 12:43

Mystery

As one thinks about the mystery of life and that of love,
You must ask some questions of the Great One up above.
One question I've been asking weighs heavy on my back.
Can you quench a love in one? Or do they take it back?
Do people have the power to reach another's heart,
Turn off the source of love, make the feelings depart?
It must not be the way of things, because if it were true,
We could also reach right in and make them love us at times too.

John 5:44

Off-Colored Shade

I wish I could say I was perfect,
A mistake I never had made. But God didn't make me angelic;
He gave me an "off-colored" shade.
So with time and some reflection,
Improvements will come by and by.
Also, your love and attention.
Oh, please let me give it a try.
Timothy 2:6-8

Treasure

Young love was like a treasure found
By two young souls, their spirits bound
By lives confused, by stress and strife.
It seemed the answer to this life.
But youth still present meant that growing
Must occur, its changes showing.
With constant upward thrust,
Their treasures lay amongst the dust.
Though time and toil have had their way,
The treasure is still there today.

Ecclesiastes 9:1

STEPS

My life did take some twists and turns
To change what it would be. At times it's hard
To take the things the Lord would send to me.
All things are said to lead to good
For those that would believe.
So I must take with loving heart
All that I may receive.
Look at my life with faithful eyes,
Believing in my soul with trust and faith.
My Lord will surely lead me to his goal.
So take my hand extended,
Lead me through this maze.
Your steps will surely lead me
To bright and blessed days.
Romans 8:28

Forgive

Love is but a feeling that must find a place.
Old fears, doubts and hurting give them chase.
You know that I am sorry; this could not be truer.
I see the pain and feel the shame for what I've done to you.
I need to have you love me, but this just will not be
Until deep inside your heart, you decide to forgive me.
Ephesians 4:32

NO THanKS

The sweet young bride, her life in stride,
At home had things to do.
She asked her man to love her as she thought he needed to.
He said, "Not now. My work is how I'll show my love to you."
On went his tasks, no questions asked,
Until his work was through.
"See, dear, my love is clear, look what I have become!"
She says, "No thanks, I will join the ranks
And do as you have done."
Ephesians 5:33
1Corinthians 7:33

SUMMIT

The mountain is very steep to climb.
A challenge great, so little time.
In haste to reach the lofty goal,
You cast aside all but your soul.
Racing headlong toward the summit,
Using care, lest you plummet.
Standing proud that you have made it.
Look again—
Find you're naked.
Proverbs 16:18

I did find someone to love and love me back. Much like a toy or tool, if you don't treat it right, it ends up broken. My relationship crashed and burned. It also flowed into my work life. Things were rough for me. Have you ever broken anything?

CHAPTER 3

Dark Days

My efforts were failing. Working hard, I would climb upon a pedestal. I found success at work, having boxes of sales awards. I also found success at home with two wonderful daughters that loved life and were easy to be proud of, as well as wife that seemed to be content with the life provided for her. A home of our own built largely by my hands. What could go wrong?

I was proud on one hand but hurting on the other.

God, I find, hates pride. It's because it takes our eyes off of Him and puts the spotlight on ourselves. God disciplines those He loves. He loved me and chose to spank me soundly—just like my earthly father—without a lot of explaining. Both God and Dad knew, with some time, the answer to the "Why me?" question would be revealed.

God kicked the pedestal out from under me. Not only once but at least three times in major areas of my life. He has done it while I am writing this book.

Praise be to God. My marriage failed, my career bottomed out, and I had health challenges. I felt pain as never before in my life. Have you been hurt too? Don't worry. That is what this life can do to you.

Bear with me in this chapter; it will probably be the longest one. As I have discovered, most poets start writing when life hurts. But that is what we need the most when we think we are in charge. Who is in charge of your life?

Blame

Sometimes I hear the stories of men whose hearts are bad.
Thoughtless words or actions make those close so sad.
I see the fruit of this as useless hurt or pain,
Done with selfish purpose that never sees a gain.
I want to point a finger to cause those men some shame.
I have done this also and need to share the blame.

1Kings 8:46
Romans 3:23

Garden

A boy once had a garden, a special place to be,
When there he felt quite happy, but lonely too, you see.
He thought he'd share this secret place
With someone he held true.
Once behind the gate, she said, "This simply will not do."
His flowers were not her favorite type,
About that open space—
She seemed to see things he had missed,
His heart began to race.
He grabbed his hoe, went to go to make his garden better!
Move this plant, remove the thatch,
Make the ground much wetter.
His queer actions caused the birds to fly.
Every plant he moved died.
Before he saw blisters on his hand,
The garden was back to bare land.
Proverbs 21:9

COLD Heart

Dear love of mine, with a heart so cold,
There is much to share, much to be told.
We've come so far, asleep and dreaming,
Quiet secrets in us steaming.
Believing things that are not true,
You thinking I did not love you.
My heart is yearning for a chance
To melt with yours in true romance.
Missing your kisses soft and warm,
Your hugs, a touch upon my arm.
We haven't been what we could be.
You must not fear, nor should you flee.
We have some living yet to do.
Please let me make things up to you.
2 Corinthians 1:9

GHOSTS

The battle raged; I thought we'd won.
A better life had now begun.
To the victor go the spoils,
Fair reward for all the toil.
On the ground, that now is gain.
The ghosts of conquered ones remain.
Psalm 66:18

Freedom

A beautiful bird once lived in a cage.
Quite secure, quite cozy, no need to rage.
The cage had no locks, a door never latched.
She sat on eggs not yet hatched,
Longing to fly out under the stars
To get past the door well out past the bars.
Devoted she stayed where she felt she belonged
Because of those lives nurtured with song.
One day in a moment, her wards take to flight,
Showing how wrong she had felt in her plight.
The cage could not hold those spirits, well-nurtured.
They took to the sky, out toward the future.
She felt free to join them, her task now completed.
As she flew out beyond, the bars now defeated,
She saw the mystery as never before—
The cage had always provided a door.
Proverbs 31:11

GUILTY HEART

Your guilt is large for acts you've done, even those
I did not see. You keep it secret, cannot set it free.
When I am blue or lonely, it only makes it worse.
Because the past replays itself, you can't undo the hurts.
If rather I behave myself, find a way to love,
You don't think you deserve it, return it with a shove.
There is no way to win this fight, without the want to change.
Look out past your guilty heart and start to rearrange.

James 2:13

Trojan Horse

This messenger has a message, needing to be said.
To deliver it in real time, causing heartfelt dread.
In the risk of verbal delivery, this message could be lost.
Mixing it in a poem might just avoid this cost.
Place it in the Trojan horse, send it through the gate,
It now becomes a loving gift. They are sure to take the bait.
Proverbs 17:27-28

converse

These poems stack up with things I wish to say.
In the time we spend together, all we do is play.
Don't get me wrong, I love these times, wanting even more.
Each time it's over, I wonder, "What's the score?"
I want to share my thoughts with you,
Sharing my last verse, having you tell me what it means,
Having you converse.
Ephesians 5:33
1 Corinthians 7:33

Lone Wolf

My heart is like a lone wolf crying at night,
Searching for his mate, alone in his plight.
He knows she went hunting alone, unlike before.
When both would share duty, their pups were cared for.
She was a good hunter when together they both went.
Loved to watch her tracking, enjoyed the time they spent.
What keeps her now that she's gone away?
Loneliness has shown what she brought to each day.
Perhaps the thrill, alone to kill, has given her glee.
Now wants to run solo to be completely free.
He lies alone and waits, his heart in pain.
Wanting to share adventure,
To be running with her again.

DC aND ME

There must have been a time now past when DC was the craze.
Once groomed, loved, and petted, those were much finer days.
But those who seemed to need him lost interest in his care,
Went on to other pleasures, did not care if he was there.
Some time ago, they left him. I don't think it was his fault.
He was just another nuisance not fitting in their vault.
You cannot know his feelings, if he blames himself somehow,
Or takes what life now gives him. It's all there is for now.
Maybe lower creatures are sheltered from the pain
When those once thought to love them
Leave them in the rain.
Ecclesiastes 7:14

There was a stray cat we adopted. In this poem, I compare this abandoned cat I called DC to my situation.

PITY ME

Our past is gone but feelings stay, move back to visit when they may.
We know not when or why they do, back they come,
Hope it's not you.
Hurts of past events come up, make old memories erupt.
You hope the pains you felt were gone,
But life again may sing those songs. I'd change that if I could,
To live the way I thought I should.
Life's not been so kind to me; I'm not what I had hoped to be.
So where from here am I to go?
This answer I would like to know.
Two girls I have, should call me dad,
Most times it feels they never had.
We're told to love people as they are,
To disregard their every scar.
Was this measure used for me,
To see me as I have to be?
Psalm 25:16

MY DAY

Some time ago I had my day,
Lived my life in my own way.
Most things I did I did for you,
To impress you with the things I do.
But for reasons not quite clear,
Actions drove you from me, dear.
It seems to be a mystery why I need you so.
There is not enough without you
For me to let you go.
1 Corinthians 7:33

LUST

Fingers flying, guilt denying, cruising through the sites.
No one looking, feeling safe. My pulse reaching new heights.
Diving deeper each time I go, needing more and more.
Surely no one can care what happens to a whore.
My eyes are pulled along like a pig to slaughter.
One more click, and to my surprise,
I am looking at your daughter!
Matthew 5:28

JUNK

Don't know for sure why I first tried it;
It was like a curious thirst.
Certain of no danger, this being my first.
The feeling was elation like I'd never felt before!
What could be so bad? I wanted even more.
The trap door closed with me inside, unable to get free.
The need for more took over, hopelessly changing me.
It's hard to live this life. The cost I cannot cover.
The only way the pain will stop
Is if I can start over.
Ecclesiastes 3:21

I'm sorry to say dark days are never completely behind us; there will
be more up ahead. It is how you choose to react or handle those days
that keeps you going. Time for us to move ahead. Still with me?

HIDDen

We Know that Jesus provides forgiving
Yet fleshly sins disrupt our living.
We fool ourselves to think we're hidden
Doing what we know is forbidden.
God has spent his heavenly wrath
While we are here on this earthly path.
He then allows our errant actions
To suffer from the laws reaction.
Correcting our misguided course
Steering us with His mighty force.
We still remain free to choose.
Without His love we only lose.
Romans 5:8

CHAPTER 4

Rebound

So we've been hurt. What do we do? We could give up or become suicidal. Or just make people think we are. This may grant us some sympathy we think we need. Take "happy pills" to cope. I did. I drank too much to drown out the pain. Or you could hand the whole mess over to God, one day at a time, then wait patiently while he restores your life—or what is left of it. I finally did the latter after all else seemed to be of no use.

As mentioned in the last chapter, my writing started during those darkest of days. It did seem to help a little. But not letting go of my crutches entirely, my efforts were still failing. I was still trying to maintain control. But my focus was slowly changing. Enough had happened that my belief in God had increased to the point that I was open to teaching. So I decided to loosen my grip on the reigns of my life, allowing myself to move forward rather than staying in my "funk" and giving up on life.

Hope you are still with me. Don't give up. The best is yet to come.

You may have noticed my references to Bible verses after the poems. Now would be a good time to read the book of Job again or for the first time. He lost it all, then God restored everything, adding even more.

sunshine and Rain

Flowers love the sunshine; they also need the rain.
Life cannot be happy if you never feel its pain.
You cannot grow on morning dew; you also need a flood.
Wars were never fought and won without the loss of blood.
So it is with life and love, there come those times of pain.
Look at it as growth to come, much like an April rain.
Romans 8:28

BURNING BRIDGES

I'm sorry that at times I'm blue,
When all I need I find in you.
I've chased the empty fleeting goals
That turned my life into worthless coals.
The little things that life may give
Is all I need for the life I live.
The path I've traveled is no more,
Your love has changed me to the core.
It's time to slow and smell the roses,
See the joy in all life's poses.
Please hold me close as I now learn
About the bridges I must burn.
Jeremiah 15:19

MIGHTY OAK

The storm came in all its fury—
Lightning, rain, evil, and worry tearing at the mighty oak. Ripping,
shredding, branches broke.
Smaller saplings could never best the awful beating sent to test.
The proud oak's strength, its purpose learning.
A place in life, some glory earning.
No one is sure why it's still standing—
All around are pieces landing.
Some think its roots grew deep and long.
During better days with sun and song.
Others say its soil held its girth,
Chosen well its place on Earth.
The storm is breaking, horrors ending, branches left cease their
bending.
Standing proud yet scarred to hell. Marks will fade but stories tell
About the strength this tree contains, that after all It still remains.
Romans 15:4

Maker

Each time our maker closes a door, He opens up a window.
Just when, or why, or where it is. It's not for us to know.
Look forward, enjoy the view, get out there if you can.
We live not in the future, cannot relive the past.
Enjoy today in every way. Make the feeling last!
2 Corinthians 4:16

one-man cart

I'm not asking you to fill the place
That now is just an empty space.
I'm making today a brand-new start
Using just a "one-man cart."
This doesn't mean I don't want you.
At times, I'll let you push it too.
I know now I am but one.
A new life has just begun.
1 Peter 5:5-7

CHILD'S TOY

I sense you think a lot of me. More than maybe I can be.
To yourself, be true. After all, your life is you.
Take the gifts that life can give. Enjoy the life only you can live.
You cannot stop the sun in the sky. Never let life pass you by.
Go after what will give you joy
Like a child with a toy.
Psalm 39:4-5

GET YOUR WAY

From one "chump" to another, some words I'd like to say.
You did your best to please them,
Even though they had their way.
The past you see much clearer, though hurts there still must be.
Now things are different. You have been set free.
Answer only to your heart. Let your spirit soar.
Be true to your feelings; they don't own you anymore.
If something's there you're wanting, go for it, my dear.
Tell yourself you're worthy. Nothing should you fear.
You own all of yourself, with no debt you need to pay.
Be everything you want to be. You may just get your way.
2Corinthians 3:15-18

Friends

Friends like you are hard to find,
Much like a precious stone.
You're always there, and you always care;
I know I'm not alone.
After spending time with you,
I like the way I feel.
It's great to have good friends like you,
So wonderful and real.
Proverbs 18:24

strayed

You strayed away for reasons clear.
Now you know, I love you, dear.
We cannot send up fallen rain,
So please don't shelter any pain.
The future lays ahead all pure.
Mistakes and pain we now can cure.
Luke 17:3

BLIND

The blind one walks with arms outstretched.
For love her heart did ache and wretch.
Hoping by chance her path would lead
To someone she thought could fill her need.
Voices heard along the way
Were spoken only to lead astray.
Loving words well-chosen and spoken
Caused the blinding spell to be broken.
Now her destiny she sees,
Walking toward love with greatest ease.
Matthew 7:15-20

WHAT'S LEFT

Your heart yearns for carefree passion
Yet is held back by guilt's action.
We've crossed the deep and wide ravine,
Learning and growing from what we've seen.
We can never drift on back
Because we see what we did lack.
Please celebrate with me, my dear.
The love you see, now that it's clear.
Don't give the past another minute—
Let's squeeze this life for what's
Left in it.
Ephesians 2:15

One Up, One Down

The past is past; today is ours.
We only have the present hours.
Blinded by youth, forward we started.
Because of love, we never parted.
One up, one down; we rocked along,
Course uncharted, onward.
On to the future, hearts maturing.
Trials shared provide us learning.
We cannot know what waits ahead,
But we can face it without dread
Because we traveled much before.
Hand in hand, each to adore.
I love you now more than ever.
Be with me here and forever.
Genesis 2:24

SHARING

My love means not that I possess you,
Only hold and gently caress you.
Sharing life as we move freely,
Meeting changes, struggles, feelings.
Accepting growth, this life arranges.
Marveling at the subtle changes.
Growing with each dawning day.
Loving all along the way.
Romans 12:9

BEHIND A CLOUD

My mind full as I meditate. For your true love,
I long, yet wait. Past pain has fallen like gentle rain.
Upon your soul, a quenching drain.
Rains come, rains go. It is the way that flowers grow.
But rain alone no blossoms bring.
The sun must shine; the birds must sing.
My love is like the sun so proud,
But sometimes it hides behind a cloud.
Clouds do pass, the sunrays now glowing.
As my love for you, its presence now showing.
It never leaves when raindrops fall.
It only hides once more to call.
The rainy days we must endure.
We cannot change this part for sure.
Please don't cry over showers past.
My love is true and sure to last.
Ephesians 5:25

So you messed up like me. Time to shake off the dust, patch up the wounds, learn a lesson or two, and start over. Hopefully you will do better. Take a mulligan, and keep moving.

PET SIN

Our pet starts out cute, warm, and fuzzy
Lots of fun; why would we worry?
We play with it and feed it. How are we to know?
With time and attention, it then begins to grow.
It goes from warm and fuzzy to big and very scary.
We cannot let it live with us it's smelling up the house.
It will not run away and hide, like a little mouse.
We need to have it go away for life to regain peace
But over many years of care; it grants us no release.
Then it's best to meet this test by calling in your "brothers,"
Them in view, Christ in you, This pest you now
May smother.
1 John 1: 7-9

CHAPTER 5

Loving Again

After the "fall and rebound," it was time to move forward. My life had changed from what it had been. I sat aside my King James Bible, the confirmation Bible referred to before, for a NIV study Bible. It was time to seek more answers.

My new beginning included a new career as an over-the-road truck driver. As a little boy, I loved trucks and any chance to take a ride with any of our family's trucker friends, of which there were several. I also loved to do pencil drawings on any scrap paper I could find. I especially loved the outdated Farm Bureau calendars, always plentiful after the new year started.

Plus, in the winter in Iowa, drawing was something to do inside. These calendars had a page for each week like a stand-up spiral notebook. On the back, if there was no farmer's almanac info or other writing, it was ready for my art. What did I like to draw, along with dinosaurs? Trucks!

Driving across the country to deliver my loads gave me the opportunity to study the Bible. Also with satellite radio, many hours

60

were spent listening to shows like *The Bible Answer Man*. Away from the major distractions in my life, these were years to heal and grow. Another area of growth was a few unwanted pounds. Watch out for snack foods!

During this time, I met a beautiful, kind, and understanding woman—unattached, I might add. We somehow seemed to be made for each other. It took twelve good years of courting to grow back my trust and change into the kind of man worthy of this woman.

She definitely had an advantage, marrying a different man than my first wife had. Not saying I've reached any level of perfection; I never will be perfect—only improved.

The same goes for you. We are always under construction like the highways we travel. Much of the old life was gone. It was time to rebuild, stronger and better, having learned a lot about what does not work.

Some of these poems are dear to me. If you see the name Nellie in my poems, this was my wife's nickname while we were courting. Some fellows have asked me if I actually gave these poems to her. No gun in my arsenal has not been fired. They must have worked. Together now as husband and wife, we are very happy, twelve years and counting.

Maybe you will find a way to tell your feelings to your most important person. Go ahead and use these if you like. As I put this chapter together, it became clear to me that no single Bible verse seemed to match what was being said, poem by poem.

Rather, one book would be a better reference to make. The book of Song of Songs in the Old Testament and chapter thirty-one of Proverbs clearly speak of what occurs between a man and a woman who are in love with each other. God intended to make love and sex to be a gift and blessing to us. No kidding. May it be a blessing to you too, if you follow His owner's manual.

FIRST GLIMPSE

This little glimpse I've had of you
Has set my heart a whirl.
So many questions I now have—
Just who are you, my girl?
I want to know just who you are.
What are you to be to me?
What do you need? Am I to lead?
What is my role to be?
Are you to be my destiny
Or just a stepping-stone?
The only thing I know for sure:
With you, I'm not alone.

Late Love

How did you stay so long alone?
Why does no one your heart now own
When you have such love to give?
You make my life one I can live.
Did you know you'd have to wait?
Or have I passed through heaven's gate?

view

Most every night, I think of you,
Your lovely face I choose to view.
If you are close, the vision's real.
When you're far away, in my memory, you appear.
You're with me everywhere I go.
No greater love I'll ever know.

DISCOVERED

Oh, Nellie dear, what have you done?
I vowed I would stay free.
I stay myself, upon the shelf,
Content to just be me.
The "Big Guy" did have a plan.
To be alone was not meant for man.
This much we know is true.
A lonely moment I've not known
Since I've discovered you.
Proverbs 18:22

comfortable

Why do I feel so comfortable with my Nellie sweet?
Why is each moment spent with her such a special treat?
Could it be those great big eyes full of care and thought?
Or her arms wrapped around me that have me caught?
Or her soft skin so clear, wanting to explore?
Or the joy felt from her laughter
That leaves me wanting more?
So many reasons I can find. She sets my spirit free.
Another one could be
She's so comfortable with me.
Song of Solomon 4:9

True

It's been so long since love was true.
Now here I am and so are you.
Can what we have be so real?
The pleasures now we both feel.
Each day needs a part of you:
Your voice, a touch, another view.
I thought I had a life before—
Since you've been here
It's so much more.

CHanGeD PLans

Oh, Nellie dear, you have to hear,
How much you changed my plan.
I was to run like wildfire,
Really be the man.
Be happy with a one-night stand,
No cares outside myself.
Take them down, dance around,
Back upon the shelf.
You did have to take it slow—
Show me to your mind.
You have saved me from much hurt
I was yet to find.
Proverbs 6:27

FLY

A new skill I've learned to do;
It is special and taught by you.
Just close my eyes,
See you close by,
Think of you—
Now I can fly!

well

Your sudden close attention has caused my heart to flow.
Where all these thoughts come from, I really do not know.
It's hard to tell if "this old well" could ever just run dry.
Please don't pumping.
It's been so fun; let's try.

GIFT PACKAGE

I've never needed a warm embrace or kiss more than now.
God wrapped them in a package and sent them to me. *Wow.*
He wrapped them with a caring soul whose heart is much too kind.
Wound it up with cords of wonder, the ends so hard to find.
Placed you in the strangest place, made it a surprise.
Now when I see it all, I can't believe my eyes.
He's been wrapping you for years and years
To make you who you are.
One thing's for sure: good friends we'll be
As we open up our gifts.
It's exciting and rewarding;
Our hearts truly lift.

TOTAL

Do not be upset, my sweetheart, if I don't notice your hair.
Do not think me unthoughtful for not noticing what you wear.
My eyes are on you always. Outside things they may not see.
They look upon your aura, see the total you would be.
I love all things about you—
Not the pieces but the whole.
Noticing the little things should also be my goal.

READING MINDS

My thoughts and yours don't always rhyme.
We think different things as we spend our time.
Some thoughts at times must be said.
Quiet minds just can't be read.
A little talk is like a food
We've been craving that tastes so good.

New Start

What force within you made you see
The things you need deep in me?
What drive empowered you to care,
Knowing now you should be there?
With your past as it has been,
What made you now begin again?
What's happened to us, Nellie girl?
Why are our lives now in a whirl?

MY EYES

Something you said to me has led me, dear, to wonder.
You said you have been very good
But are worried about your blunder.
I then would ask what acts you have been prone to do
That you now feel should not be part of you?
We cannot be our total selves, holding too much back.
Try reading the paper, leaving out the black
Relax a bit, take a risk, and you may be surprised
What you would be, if you could see,
Yourself through my two eyes.

SLEEPLESS

Oh, Nellie dear, it warms my heart, to know I'm in your head.
That an evening chat stirs you so, it's hard to go to bed.
I hope first morning's light
Still finds me on your mind.
To find a soul that enjoys me so
Was what I'd hoped to find.

GOLD

Like precious gold in a mountain vein
The love in your heart does remain.
Waiting for the eager soul
To stake his claim and seek his goal.
To mine the treasure of your love
To bring you out and up above.
The world can now see the treasure
That none before could ever measure.

Fear

Just the act of meeting frightened you at first.
Letting down your guard was even worse.
Telling me your feelings caused you some dread,
Allowing me to know what goes on in your head.
Our bike adventure scared you to death,
Thinking at times you had drawn your last breath.
Fear can have its place as a useful thing,
As long as it does not quench the joy life can bring.
Hold my hand, Nellie, let me take you there.
Nothing can harm you. I truly care.

BUTTErFLY

Nellie is my butterfly just out of her cocoon.
Just what her colors are to be, it's still a little soon.
Her wings are still spreading out, not completely dry.
You can see it in her eyes; she wants so much to fly.
I cannot wait either. So beautiful she'll be.
Flying after oh so long.
Flying straight to me.

Giver

Your whole life you chose to give.
It was the way you liked to live.
You felt with time, things would return.
That love from others you are sure to earn.
Time did pass with little gain,
Joyful giving turns to pain.
Gifts you give, but you're no receiver.
If life's fair, you're no believer.
God's great scale is always true;
He sent me to give to you.
Matthew 10:42

WOOD

I did not want to care so much—not like this, my dear.
With oh so many feelings, way too little fear.
What's happened to my strength, to guard my fragile soul,
To focus on my selfish needs, to run for the next goal?
Was it your eyes fixed firm on mine like mirrors to my heart?
Or your sweet tears, mixing with mine,
That tore me all apart? Or your desire to light a fire
Because you knew you could? Because I was just some kindling,
Would you be the wood?

Drama

How can it be that I could see your thoughts behind your eyes?
Or know there was my Nellie behind a thin disguise?
Why has my heart melted? It seems to mix with yours.
Time we spend together, minutes turn to hours.
Lyrics to a special song, sung with both our hearts.
Each act our lives are playing out.
We are perfect for the parts.

MY WIFE, THE GIVER

If devotion ran the scoreboard or selflessness earned a prize,
I see a mighty champion here before my eyes.
Your love shines like the brilliant sun, warming those you see.
You use your power every hour, giving without fee.
Like the sun, you cannot hide your willingness to please.
To have you as a part of me sets my heart at ease.
Proverbs 31

FIXer

Someone hurt you, Nellie, my dear.
I do not want to; I hope that's clear.
I'm not the only one with healing to do.
We both need fixing; isn't that true?
I'm a good fixer, if you'll just hold still.
Fix all I can, not send you a bill.
All I ask is set yourself free.
Allow yourself to grow closer to me.

Paths Crossed

Our paths have crossed; this much is done.
Two minds have met. The dance begun.
No one can tell the rhythm, or will the music end?
Let us enjoy the music—
Let our spirits mend.

VISION

I used to lie in bed at night, wishing for what was gone.
Trying to change the past, undoing what was wrong.
Now it's very different. The past I do not see.
A whole new vision greets my sight.
It's you, dear, here with me.
I see your face in pale moonlight,
Your eyes a welcome sight.
Seeking out my essence, exploring me tonight.
Sleep is still elusive; it finds me hard to tame.
Life is much more pleasant. It's become a different game.

Trust

Your reaction to the lady fair
Who chose to draw too near
Has made my mind quite puzzled
To what you seem to fear.
Could it be a lack of self esteem
That you doubt what you would be?
Or fear her crafty methods
That she could spellbind me?
Perhaps my selfish habits
Have caused your trust to wane,
Wondering what my heart contains
That cause you now this pain.

OLD STORY

I told the story to you, dear, about the past.
Did you hear? About how I was a "fixer."
A lonely, hungry, heart "jinxer?"
Once she was well and had her way,
She turned from me to run away.
Part of me sees things the same
Fears inside you need to tame.
Show me how wrong I am,
How the past was just a scam.
Show me how one can love true.
How it might just be you.

scared

I'm scaring you, Nellie. What can it be?
Do you think it's demons hidden in me?
Or is the fear something in you
Afraid of things you don't want to do?
Think of the brave and the mountains they climb
Or the chances I take sharing these rhymes.
It's terribly frightful to do the unknown.
Choke down the fear; let courage be shown.
I think there are two Nellies:
One mild and meek, another one hidden
I'm hoping to meet.

your flowers

I'm sure you've seen other's flowers on special days arrive,
Had to say they are pretty and smile to survive.
Today's your day, my Nellie, to even up the score.
For there is someone out here, and you he does adore.
Make sure they all can see them; I hope they last awhile.
Sit back, enjoy, think of me. Watch the other's smile.

MY Name

The way I feel I cannot explain; it goes beyond the norm.
Making you so happy makes my heart so warm.
I know you've not asked for this; I give it just the same.
Sit back, reflect, and you'll understand.
Give this love my name.

WEDDING RING

Our lives until now have not been the best.
We set out now to live the rest.
A better path we now will try,
Our lives now clear as springtime sky.
Begin with me a life of joy.
May each day be a treasured toy.
The love you need to you I bring.
Please wear with pride my wedding ring.

Lovely woman

No woman is lovelier than the one beside me now.
No bride in white, no classy tripe, no matter where or how.
She's stood beside me always, through all that life has brought.
She loves and shares, she always cares, is always in my thoughts.
She is my love, my treasured dove;
I'll always want her near.
My heart cries out with words of love
I hope her heart can hear.

You can see that chapter did exceed the volume of the dark days. This should be a good sign. There is much more love and hope than pain and misery if we look in the right places with a proper state of mind. Stay with me now as we move from our love for our spouse to how God feels toward us.

CHAPTER 6

God's True Nature

I am over the peak of the mountain of despair. Life looks much different than it did not so long ago. There are sure to be many more challenges ahead. This time, however, I know that I do not need to face them alone. I have two major partners: my wife and my God.

During my darkest days, my thoughts were that God, because He knows everything, was punishing me. This is not His nature. He loves His creation and does choose at times to discipline us because of that love.

Our relationship with our spouse is an example of His relationship with us. We need to have three legs on a stool for it to stand up correctly. If you only have two, it tips over. With four, unless each leg is exactly the right length, it will wobble. You need three, and it will stand on any surface solidly. What are the three legs? They are you, your spouse, and God. God himself says He is three yet one—Father, Son, and Spirit.

This is a mystery, and our human minds cannot understand this side of heaven. Try seeing yourself explaining to a caterpillar

94

what life will be like when he becomes a butterfly. There have been countless books and other resources over centuries trying to give us understanding.

I made use of my church's library after joining. Devouring the resources there helped me answer my questions about God's creation and message. The more I thought I knew, the more I realized what was still unknown to me. This church body, Charles City E-Free City in Charles Iowa with pastor Mike Downey also has study groups that gather together to share and learn outside of its regular services.

A new life event was also discovered: Bible camp. Each January, several hundred men gather at Hidden Acres, a Christian camp, to worship, learn, and find fellowship together. These weekends helped me grow greatly.

As with everything in this small book, my desire for you is to whet your appetite for more learning and growth. You can find others wherever you live to join with you. Also, today with the internet, information abounds. Watch out for false prophets who want things for themselves. God does like prayers for wisdom and discernment. Go ahead and ask.

Let's now move closer to God exploring what he wants to show us.

Train to Salvation

I am riding on a train on my way to a wedding feast.
I'm surprised I was invited; I thought I was the least.
The trip could take some time it stops again and again.
To pick up those invited that want to give up sin.
The ride when interrupted is a joy though, just the same.
The only darkness noted are those that still remain.
The train is large-with many seats,
We hope the host will fill.
There is one right beside me where I pray he puts Bill.
When the day does come when we arrive
We will celebrate with endless joy; that we are still alive.
Matthew 22: 1-14

GOD'S CLOCK

God's clock upon His wall measures time that he created.
Spinning around with his attention, running in each direction.
We want badly to control it, turn it back when we feel sad.
Push it forward, thinking we would then be glad.
Sit back with trust. Enjoy this time He has made to be.
Give thanks that we can do this
Now through eternity.
2 Peter 3:8

Traveler

The young man had not traveled far, but enough that he was
knowing
That glancing back upon his tracks, he had some help while going.
It was not luck or chance when things would go his way
Or his own strength bringing him through a darker day.
He chanced upon an older man with his gray head of glory.
He took some time to share with him about his travel story.
The older man listened lovingly to the young man's tale
About how God was now and then "pulling back the veil."
He then said, "Young man, let me share with you my story
About how God has shown to me his everlasting glory.
God does not come and go on days you think you need him
Or show up when you think you have pleased him.
He was with you every inch you've traveled to get here,
And he's on the trail ahead. Go, my son, don't fear."

Joshua 1:5

Grandpa

Upon his lap his grandson rests; Grandpa feels pure joy.
Caring for his "little man" who's still a little boy.
Not content to stay in place, a battle starts to rage,
Stemming from the boy at a very tender age.
Wishing to flee to find his glee, doing as he pleases.
Grandpa holding on, loving as he squeezes.
He wins because he loves him. Also, he is stronger.
Just like God does for us
When we choose to wander.
Jeremiah 3:4

WEDDING FEAST

We are invited to a party; it looks to be quite grand.
We needn't travel very far; it's right here in our land.
For some reason, most refuse to go.
The true excuse does not show.
Their own needs seem more important.
At home they choose to stay.
Burning the invitations, going their own way.
If we heard the true reason,
They would not want to boast.
They simply are all selfish
And also hate the host!
Matthew 22:1-15

Never Alone

Each one was placed upon this earth, not meant to be alone.
Father, mother, sister, brother, mates of flesh and bone.
Then we leave; next, to cleave to the mate God made for us.
Another family claims us too: Christ's body of believers.
Unlike the others, they stay true.
Never will they leave us.
Proverbs 27: 10

GOD'S NEW VESSEL

This earthly vessel we've become by living selfishly
Falls off the shelf into the blood our Savior shed for thee.
The life we made with manly flesh slowly melts away,
Rising again to spin anew and be the potter's clay.
Godly hands replacing man's; this new vessel will be glorious.
Spinning at His will, letting Him restore us.
Its glazing will show God's glory; the handle will fit His hands.
Pouring out useful works, designed to fulfill His plans.
Isaiah 64:8

GOD LOVED US FIRST

God loved us first; the Bible's true.
He loves me; he loves you.
You'd want to please him if you could.
Your guilty heart says you should,
For all the grace He's freely shown.
The power to pay you do not own.
Accept the gifts He's chosen to give.
Relax in Christ.
You now can live!
John 3:16

LITTLE FRUIT

Why would I ever deserve wrath? What I do is not so bad.
No murder, rape, or thievery. No taxes do I pad.
Looking out at the crazy world,
Comparing them to me, the scale would never level out.
A difference I do see.
But truth be told, in tales of old,
To the garden we return.
What did Adam do so bad that the curse this earth did earn?
What sin was it that angered God to earn his leather suit?
He ignored God, had his way,
And ate a little fruit.
1 John 1:8

THE LORD'S ARMS

The little boy with knee scuffed up,
His mother he is seeking.
Tears and fears welling up,
Searching as he's weeping.
Mother found, her love surrounds
The little boy in pain.
A kiss, a hug, a tender word,
She shows her love again.
We also cry to God above
When life causes us harm.
We gain comfort from our Lord,
Nestled in his arms.
Psalms 71:21

creator

God made us in his image,
His nature we all share.
He made us with all other things
On earth and in the air.
God surely has joy
Watching what he made,
From flowers in the desert
To critters in the shade.
We also get excited, making things too,
Working on an idea, showing something new.
Be careful with your pride
When your creation you now gauge.
You didn't create anything;
You only rearranged.
John 1:3

Teeter Totter

In the middle of the playground, the teeter totter resides.
We answer Gods calling, hopping on one side.
God is on the other, waiting to ascend.
Without some holy help, the ride will surely end.
To raise God up, He sends His Son to our weaker side.
With His great weight, we then begin the ride.
One trip down is all we do.
God goes up; Jesus with you.
One life it takes to make the trip down.
The lower you go, the greater joy will be found.
Matthew 19:26

GOD'S JOHNNY APPLESEED

Johnny had a vision in his heart.
The world needed more apples.
This is his task to do.
Like our driven Johnny, there is more this world needs,
Along with juicy apples planted with his seeds.
God's word, through this message,
May plant His Spirit's seeds.
Growing the gospel message
Rather than fruit trees.
Romans 10:14-15

vengeance

Vengeance is mine sayeth the Lord.
These words we know are true.
Easier said than done when this hurt
Would come to you.
A fool told me my vengeance would be
When joy returned one day.
After years of tears, it came to me.
Now I'm happily on my way.
To flaunt it at my oppressor
Would be payback now for me.
Peace cannot be complete if this is now to be.
My heart tells me a much better way to go.
To pray my dear Lord gives them
This happiness I know.
Deuteronomy 32:35

PaTH

The path of my life came very close to the gates of glory.
What a life-changing chapter to this part of my story.
Why am I still here, not led to cross over,
To meet my sweet Jesus,
Rest in heaven's clover?
Was this discipline sent from above,
To change me even more because of your love?
So I remain here in this crazy circus,
Looking for direction to fulfill your purpose.
I know not the steps. I am only a man
Moving in His direction, His word as my guide.
Hope as my fuel, His spirit inside.
Proverbs 20:24

Heaven's Hound

The holy hound of heaven out of glory came for me,
Chased me without ceasing, never let me be.
I ran away with all the strength my sinful heart could muster.
I fled through sin, pride, things with earthly luster.
Fearing if He reached me, I'd suffer from His wrath.
Then I fell below a cross he'd placed along my path,
Falling in a pool of blood below it, shed for me,
Dripping from the Savior
Who took this wrath for me.
Psalms 85:2-3

THE END

Our lives will reach an ending; this is a godly rule.
How you do it, when it comes,
You cannot learn in school.
Some go slow, others quickly
Or sadly by their hand.
To reach the end with peaceful joy
Is what the Lord has planned.
To reach this goal, you give your soul
To Him who chose to make it.
Don't fool yourself with fame or wealth
To think that you can fake it.
Luke 1:79

DISTANCE

I long for my dear grandkids so far away from me.
Longing to share your story, them perched upon my knee.
Distance keeps us separated. Your love I cannot share.
You love them even more than me
I leave them in your care.
Isaiah 41:13

Break the Chains

I now look out at others, see how they run free.
Envy how they make new plans and wish it could be me.
Duty keeps me anchored, doing what I must.
Wanting what they must enjoy
At times I almost bust.
To break the chains would create pains
To those I truly love.
Give me the strength to go the length
Serving those you love.
Ephesians 4:11-13

DOCTOr

Years of school and spending on your way
To a life of mending, a task not many bear.
Your hope would be every patient would heal
After your good care. To be honest and realistic,
The best care that you could give
Will only add some extension to the days that they may live.
Though what you do is noble, the result is much like mine.
We have very little left to show at the end of life's long line.
We hope that something's left behind to show that we were here.
A cure, a cause, or message those left behind may hear.
God tells us all is done in vain, if we only serve ourselves.
Days of our lives, like merchandise, leave only empty shelves.
If while we work, we keep in mind, our Saviors great commission,
The end of our life will leave a glorious new vision.
Souls we touched as we work, now on their way to glory,
Would be a better ending to what would be our story.
John 6:27

Teacher

I tried to teach you what I could,
But I had much to learn.
Weak was I and short of days.
Your trust I did not earn.
As a godly guide, I have no pride;
I did not do my part.
Your souls are stolen by my foe with evil in his heart.
I pray each day you go your way.
Time will erase the score.
I leave you in the hands of God
Who loves you all the more.
2 Corinthians

God does indeed erase our losing score in this game of life. Accept His free gift of grace given through the sacrifice of Jesus on the cross. Believe in His promises and repent, which means to change direction. Once you do this, you are on your way.

CHAPTER 7

The New Walk

God has given you many unique gifts. He does not need to change you into someone different for your life to matter. You were made to be yourself. He takes your broken parts, your good parts, and your past to make the future better. The future may not be perfect by worldly standards, but it will be the best by His standards. He has His plan to fulfill. Your best life is the one He planned. Once you surrender your control and accept His guidance, things will work out better than you would have expected.

For example, I have spent a big part of my life in my workshop. It is not a large shop, but it works well for repairing lawnmowers, snow blowers, and other small gas-powered items. Over the years, I collected parts left over from units that get scrapped out. One pile was rear-end transmissions. They are still useful but very seldom ever needed. For some reason, I got the crazy idea to turn them into little airplanes that could be used to entertain youngsters.

With no grandkids close by or neighborhood children, this indeed seemed crazy. However, God took my gifts and leftover parts, putting both to use. At about this time, Hope for Life pregnancy center was started in Charles City. Iowa. Putting the two together, I set up a 501c3 calling it Our Saviour's Squadron.

I loaded up the squad and headed out to local parades and town festivals, giving little "pilots" rides while sharing information about the services Hope for Life could provide for the young mothers. The towns and other sponsors paid for the entertainment value of the ride. The kids loved the planes—lots of moving parts, some sound effects, and they were not riders but "pilots." It was fun to watch them "light up" when we get going.

God has been very good to me, so we have been able to forward almost all the money raised to the center. If you are curious, you can see some videos and pictures of the squad on Facebook.

As you see in this example, God took my gift, some broken equipment and past blessings, and brought them together in His bigger plan to accomplish a greater good. You have your gifts that can do things only you can do. Offer these things up to Him, and you will be amazed at what returns. It's an exciting way to live.

God is not done with me yet. You are obviously alive if you are reading this, so he is not done with you either. You may feel broken down in a broken world. Fear not. We have a Savior. If you have not decided how to enter eternity, I pray you will. Let him guide your life, writing chapters in your book that I look forward to reading when we meet someday in heaven. Thank you for letting me share my story with you. God bless you.

ABOUT THE AUTHOR

Glenn was born in Franklin county Iowa in 1956. Graduating from Dows High School in 1974. The bulk of his continuing education was through the school of hard knocks.

His work career involved farming, steel consruction, millwright, sales, and over-the-road trucking. He has two daughters Lisa Rheinberg and Lori Lewis. Five grand children Jeremiah and Julie Lewis, Ben, Lexi, and Harry Rheinberg. Currently retired living in Osage, Iowa with his wife Bev. Glenn stays busy in his workshop if not out working with Our Saviour's Squadron or other ministries.

Made in USA - Kendallville, IN
65742_9798825287089
08.11.2022 1303